2025 PLANNER

By His Grace

FOR WOMEN LIVING IN FAITH, GRACE AND PURPOSE

C. G. Lewis

THIS PLANNER BELONGS TO

_____

Faithful Steps

Welcome to the "By His Grace" 2025 Goals Planner. This planner has been crafted to stand as your faithful companion, guiding you along the path to success. Setting and pursuing goals is not merely a personal endeavor; it is a powerful expression of faith, and we are honored to walk beside you on this journey.

As you turn the pages of this planner, envision each line as a prayerful stepping stone toward your God-inspired aspirations. The road ahead may twist and turn, marked by highs and lows, but always remember: it's not about achieving worldly perfection; it's about making progress aligned with His divine plan. Embrace this journey with a heart full of gratitude, celebrating the small victories and learning from every experience as a testament to God's grace.

This year is a unique canvas, divinely awaiting the manifestation of your dreams. Within this planner, you'll discover the tools and guidance to help you articulate your goals, break them down into actionable steps, and witness the faith-filled progression of your journey. Your presence here is not only a commitment to yourself and your vision; it's a statement that 2025 is a year of significance, growth, and accomplishment anchored in your faith.

As you walk through this faith-infused planner to support the story of grace and good success, remember your goals are a part of a divine map leading you toward a future designed by His wisdom. As you continue your journey of faith, let's dive into 2025 and make it your most spiritually enriching and successful year yet.

Dream, Plan, Achieve

How to Make the Most of Your Planner

This planner has been carefully crafted to guide you to set, achieve and celebrate your goals. Follow these three essential steps to make your goal-setting experience impactful:

1. Goal Setting Essentials
   - Identify Your Goals: Write down your dreams, no matter how big or small.
   - Prioritize What Matters Most: Focus on the goals that will have the greatest impact.
   - Action-Oriented Plans: Break each goal down into actionable tasks that keep you moving forward.

2. Preparation for Your Breakthrough
   - Affirm Daily Success: Boost your mindset with daily affirmations that align with your goals.
   - Set Clear Monthly Intentions: Choose a focus for each month to guide your journey.
   - Align Habits with Success: Schedule habits that support your personal and professional growth.
   - Reflect Monthly: Review your wins and lessons learned to stay on track for the upcoming months.

3. Celebrate Big
   - Celebrate All Your Wins: Take time to recognize every victory, big or small.
   - Measure Your Growth: Reflect on your progress and acknowledge how far you've come.
   - Embrace Lessons: Use your learnings as stepping stones to future success.
   - Practice Presence: Stay mindful of the journey, savoring each moment of growth.
   - Lessons Learned: Use your learnings as stepping stones to success.
   - Practice Presence: Stay mindful of the journey, savoring each moment of growth.

"For I know the plans I have for you, plans to prosper you and not to harm you, plans to give you hope and a future."

Jeremiah 29:11

MY VISION BOARD

Harness the power of vision boards to transform your dreams and convert your aspirations into concrete goals, shaping the life you wish to lead. Vision boards serve are dynamic tools that clarify your intentions, enhance motivation, and keep your objectives at the forefront of your mind.

WHAT I'D LIKE TO ATTRACT

SPIRITUALITY

PHYSICAL HEALTH

SELF LOVE

MY FAMILY

MONEY MINDSET

MY BIG GOAL

MY GOALS

6 MONTHS

- [ ]
- [ ]
- [ ]
- [ ]
- [ ]
- [ ]
- [ ]

1 YEAR

- [ ]
- [ ]
- [ ]
- [ ]
- [ ]
- [ ]
- [ ]

3 YEARS

- [ ]
- [ ]
- [ ]
- [ ]
- [ ]
- [ ]
- [ ]

5 YEARS

- [ ]
- [ ]
- [ ]
- [ ]
- [ ]
- [ ]
- [ ]

10 YEARS

- [ ]
- [ ]
- [ ]
- [ ]
- [ ]
- [ ]
- [ ]

LIFE GOALS

- [ ]
- [ ]
- [ ]
- [ ]
- [ ]
- [ ]
- [ ]

MY PRIORITY MATRIX

Evaluating and prioritizing your objectives ensures that you focus your energy on what matters most. By clarifying your priorities, you can allocate your time and resources effectively, paving the way for meaningful progress and success.

IMPORTANT	*Do Later*	*Do Now*
NOT IMPORTANT	*Delete*	*Delegate*

MY NOTES

_____

_____

_____

_____

MY GOAL ACTION PLAN

MY GOAL	GOAL ACTION STEPS
	☐ -------------------------------
	☐ -------------------------------
	☐ -------------------------------
MY WHY	☐ -------------------------------
	☐ -------------------------------
	☐ -------------------------------
	☐ -------------------------------
MY REWARD	DUE DATE

MY GOAL	GOAL ACTION STEPS
	☐ -------------------------------
	☐ -------------------------------
	☐ -------------------------------
MY WHY	☐ -------------------------------
	☐ -------------------------------
	☐ -------------------------------
	☐ -------------------------------
MY REWARD	DUE DATE

MY GOAL ACTION PLAN

MY GOAL

MY WHY

MY REWARD

GOAL ACTION STEPS

☐ --------------------------------
☐ --------------------------------
☐ --------------------------------
☐ --------------------------------
☐ --------------------------------
☐ --------------------------------
☐ --------------------------------

DUE DATE

MY GOAL

MY WHY

MY REWARD

GOAL ACTION STEPS

☐ --------------------------------
☐ --------------------------------
☐ --------------------------------
☐ --------------------------------
☐ --------------------------------
☐ --------------------------------
☐ --------------------------------

DUE DATE

MY GOAL ACTION PLAN

MY GOAL

MY WHY

MY REWARD

GOAL ACTION STEPS

- [ ] ------------------------------------
- [ ] ------------------------------------
- [ ] ------------------------------------
- [ ] ------------------------------------
- [ ] ------------------------------------
- [ ] ------------------------------------
- [ ] ------------------------------------

DUE DATE

MY GOAL

MY WHY

MY REWARD

GOAL ACTION STEPS

- [ ] ------------------------------------
- [ ] ------------------------------------
- [ ] ------------------------------------
- [ ] ------------------------------------
- [ ] ------------------------------------
- [ ] ------------------------------------
- [ ] ------------------------------------

DUE DATE

MY GOAL ACTION PLAN

MY GOAL

GOAL ACTION STEPS

☐ ------------------------------------
☐ ------------------------------------
☐ ------------------------------------
☐ ------------------------------------
☐ ------------------------------------
☐ ------------------------------------
☐ ------------------------------------

MY WHY

MY REWARD

DUE DATE

MY GOAL

GOAL ACTION STEPS

☐ ------------------------------------
☐ ------------------------------------
☐ ------------------------------------
☐ ------------------------------------
☐ ------------------------------------
☐ ------------------------------------
☐

MY WHY

MY REWARD

DUE DATE

MY AFFIRMATIONS

Positive affirmations are essential to making improvements in your life. Three tips:
1. Always use the present tense and the pronoun "I."
2. Use affirmative, positive language and avoid negative words such as "can't or won't" For example, "I am energetic and always take action" instead of "I am not lazy."
3. Develop a habit of using these affirmations when you find yourself doing the opposite of what you know you should be doing.

Relationships
example: "I'm loving and giving in my relationships". "I'm in control of the people I let in my life."

Finance
example: "I'm capable of creating my dream financial life through hard work and dedication."

Career
example: "I'm always striving to develop myself professionally."

Health/Fitness
example: "I'm in control of my mental and physical health."

Love
example: "I have people who love me."

MY 2025 FOCUS

Begin your year with Intention.

Date	Intention

Annual goals	Positive Visualization

Things to Learn	Acts of Kindness

GRATITUDE

2025

2025

hello

2025

JAN

S	M	T	W	T	F	S
		1	2	3	4	
5	6	7	8	9	10	11
12	13	14	15	16	17	18
19	20	21	22	23	24	25
26	27	28	29	30	31	

FEB

S	M	T	W	T	F	S
						1
2	3	4	5	6	7	8
9	10	11	12	13	14	15
16	17	18	19	20	21	22
23	24	25	26	27	28	

MAR

S	M	T	W	T	F	S
						1
2	3	4	5	6	7	8
9	10	11	12	13	14	15
16	17	18	19	20	21	22
23	24	25	26	27	28	29
30	31					

APR

S	M	T	W	T	F	S
		1	2	3	4	5
6	7	8	9	10	11	12
13	14	15	16	17	18	19
20	21	22	23	24	25	26
27	28	29	30			

MAY

S	M	T	W	T	F	S
				1	2	3
4	5	6	7	8	9	10
11	12	13	14	15	16	17
18	19	20	21	22	23	24
25	26	27	28	29	30	31

JUN

S	M	T	W	T	F	S
1	2	3	4	5	6	7
8	9	10	11	12	13	14
15	16	17	18	19	20	21
22	23	24	25	26	27	28
29	30					

JUL

S	M	T	W	T	F	S
		1	2	3	4	5
6	7	8	9	10	11	12
13	14	15	16	17	18	19
20	21	22	23	24	25	26
27	28	29	30	31		

AUG 10

S	M	T	W	T	F	S
					1	2
3	4	5	6	7	8	9
10	11	12	13	14	15	16
17	18	19	20	21	22	23
24	25	26	27	28	29	30
31						

SEP

S	M	T	W	T	F	S
	1	2	3	4	5	6
7	8	9	10	11	12	13
14	15	16	17	18	19	20
21	22	23	24	25	26	27
28	29	30				

OCT

S	M	T	W	T	F	S
			1	2	3	4
5	6	7	8	9	10	11
12	13	14	15	16	17	18
19	20	21	22	23	24	25
26	27	28	29	30	31	

NOV

S	M	T	W	T	F	S
						1
2	3	4	5	6	7	8
9	10	11	12	13	14	15
16	17	18	19	20	21	22
23	24	25	26	27	28	29
30						

DEC

S	M	T	W	T	F	S
	1	2	3	4	5	6
7	8	9	10	11	12	13
14	15	16	17	18	19	20
21	22	23	24	25	26	27
28	29	30	31			

15

"Commit to the Lord whatever you do, and He will establish your plans."

Proverbs 16:3

MY JANUARY FOCUS

Begin your month with Intention.

Date	Intention
_____	_____

Annual goals	Positive Visualization

Things to Learn	Acts of Kindness

GRATITUDE

_____

_____

_____

JANUARY 2025

SUNDAY	MONDAY	TUESDAY	WEDNESDAY
			1 New Years Day Kwanzaa
5	6	7	8
12	13	14	15
19	20 MLK Day	21	22
26	27	28	29

THURSDAY	FRIDAY	SATURDAY	TO-DO LIST
2	3	4	
9	10	11	
16	17	18	
23	24	25	
30	31		

"Commit to the Lord whatever you do, and He will establish your plans." Proverbs 16:3

19

MY WEEKLY PLANNER

MONDAY	
TUESDAY	
WEDNESDAY	
THURSDAY	
FRIDAY	
SATURDAY	
SUNDAY	

MY NOTES

TO DO

-
-
-
-
-
-
-
-
-
-
-
-

20

MY WEEKLY PLANNER

MONDAY	
TUESDAY	
WEDNESDAY	
THURSDAY	
FRIDAY	
SATURDAY	
SUNDAY	

MY NOTES

TO DO

-
-
-
-
-
-
-
-
-
-
-
-

MY WEEKLY PLANNER

MONDAY	
TUESDAY	
WEDNESDAY	
THURSDAY	
FRIDAY	
SATURDAY	
SUNDAY	

MY NOTES

TO DO

-
-
-
-
-
-
-
-
-
-
-
-
-
-

MY WEEKLY PLANNER

MONDAY	
TUESDAY	
WEDNESDAY	
THURSDAY	
FRIDAY	
SATURDAY	
SUNDAY	

MY NOTES

TO DO

-
-
-
-
-
-
-
-
-
-
-
-

MY WEEKLY PLANNER

MONDAY

TUESDAY

WEDNESDAY

THURSDAY

FRIDAY

SATURDAY

SUNDAY

MY NOTES

TO DO

-
-
-
-
-
-
-
-
-
-
-
-

MY HABIT TRACKER

Cultivate positive change with this habit tracker. Log your daily habits for the month to stay focused and committed to achieving your goals. Fostering consistency and accountability helps to paves your path toward your aspirations

MONTH _____

HABIT:

1	2	3	4	5	6	7
8	9	10	11	12	13	14
15	16	17	18	19	20	21
22	23	24	25	26	27	28
29	30	31				

HABIT:

1	2	3	4	5	6	7
8	9	10	11	12	13	14
15	16	17	18	19	20	21
22	23	24	25	26	27	28
29	30	31				

HABIT:

1	2	3	4	5	6	7
8	9	10	11	12	13	14
15	16	17	18	19	20	21
22	23	24	25	26	27	28
29	30	31				

HABIT:

1	2	3	4	5	6	7
8	9	10	11	12	13	14
15	16	17	18	19	20	21
22	23	24	25	26	27	28
29	30	31				

HABIT:

1	2	3	4	5	6	7
8	9	10	11	12	13	14
15	16	17	18	19	20	21
22	23	24	25	26	27	28

HABIT:

1	2	3	4	5	6	7
8	9	10	11	12	13	14
15	16	17	18	19	20	21
22	23	24	25	26	27	28

MY JANUARY REFLECTION

WHAT WENT WELL THIS MONTH?

WHAT DIDN'T GO SO WELL?

WHAT DID I DO FOR MY PHYSICAL AND MENTAL HEALTH THIS PAST MONTH?

1.
1.
3.
4.

WHAT AM I SPENDING TOO LITTLE AND TOO MUCH TIME ON?

WHAT AREAS OF MY LIFE DID I GROW THE MOST IN?

WHAT HAPPENED THIS MONTH MAKE ME FEEL THE MOST GRATEFUL?

1.
1.
3.
4.

WHAT CAN I ADJUST NEXT MONTH?

MY NOTES

"Write the vision
And make it plain...
That he may run who
reads it."

Habakkuk 2:2

MY FEBRUARY FOCUS

Begin your month with Intention.

Date	Intention
_____	_____

Annual goals	Positive Visualization

Things to Learn	Acts of Kindness

GRATITUDE

_____

_____

_____

February 2025

SUNDAY	MONDAY	TUESDAY	WEDNESDAY
		Black History Month	
2	3	4	5
9	10	11	12
16	17	18	19
23	24	25	26

THURSDAY	FRIDAY	SATURDAY	TO-DO LIST
		1	
6	7	8	
13	14	15	
20	21	22	
27	28		

"Write the vision and make it plain... That he may run who reads it." Habakkuk 2:2

31

MY WEEKLY PLANNER

MONDAY	
TUESDAY	
WEDNESDAY	
THURSDAY	
FRIDAY	
SATURDAY	
SUNDAY	

MY NOTES

TO DO

-
-
-
-
-
-
-
-
-
-
-
-

MY WEEKLY PLANNER

MONDAY	
TUESDAY	
WEDNESDAY	
THURSDAY	
FRIDAY	
SATURDAY	
SUNDAY	

MY NOTES

TO DO

-
-
-
-
-
-
-
-
-
-
-
-

MY WEEKLY PLANNER

MONDAY	
TUESDAY	
WEDNESDAY	
THURSDAY	
FRIDAY	
SATURDAY	
SUNDAY	

MY NOTES

TO DO

-
-
-
-
-
-
-
-
-
-
-
-

MY WEEKLY PLANNER

MONDAY	
TUESDAY	
WEDNESDAY	
THURSDAY	
FRIDAY	
SATURDAY	
SUNDAY	

MY NOTES

TO DO

-
-
-
-
-
-
-
-
-
-
-
-

MY WEEKLY PLANNER

MONDAY

TUESDAY

WEDNESDAY

THURSDAY

FRIDAY

SATURDAY

SUNDAY

MY NOTES

TO DO

-
-
-
-
-
-
-
-
-
-
-
-

MY HABIT TRACKER

Cultivate positive change with this habit tracker. Log your daily habits for the month to stay focused and committed to achieving your goals. Fostering consistency and accountability helps to paves your path toward your aspirations

MONTH _____

HABIT:

1	2	3	4	5	6	7
8	9	10	11	12	13	14
15	16	17	18	19	20	21
22	23	24	25	26	27	28
29	30	31				

HABIT:

1	2	3	4	5	6	7
8	9	10	11	12	13	14
15	16	17	18	19	20	21
22	23	24	25	26	27	28
29	30	31				

HABIT:

1	2	3	4	5	6	7
8	9	10	11	12	13	14
15	16	17	18	19	20	21
22	23	24	25	26	27	28
29	30	31				

HABIT:

1	2	3	4	5	6	7
8	9	10	11	12	13	14
15	16	17	18	19	20	21
22	23	24	25	26	27	28
29	30	31				

HABIT:

1	2	3	4	5	6	7
8	9	10	11	12	13	14
15	16	17	18	19	20	21
22	23	24	25	26	27	28

HABIT:

1	2	3	4	5	6	7
8	9	10	11	12	13	14
15	16	17	18	19	20	21
22	23	24	25	26	27	28

MY FEBRUARY REFLECTION

WHAT WENT WELL THIS MONTH?

WHAT DIDN'T GO SO WELL?

WHAT DID I DO FOR MY PHYSICAL AND MENTAL HEALTH THIS PAST MONTH?

1.
1.
3.
4.

WHAT AM I SPENDING TOO LITTLE AND TOO MUCH TIME ON?

WHAT AREAS OF MY LIFE DID I GROW THE MOST IN?

WHAT HAPPENED THIS MONTH MAKE ME FEEL THE MOST GRATEFUL?

1.
1.
3.
4.

WHAT CAN I ADJUST NEXT MONTH?

MY NOTES

"May the favor of the Lord our God rest on us; establish the work of our hands for us yes, establish the work of our hands."

Psalm 90:17

MY MARCH FOCUS

Begin your month with Intention.

Date	Intention
_____	_____

Annual goals	Positive Visualization
Things to Learn	Acts of Kindness

GRATITUDE

_____

_____

_____

_____

March 2025

SUNDAY	MONDAY	TUESDAY	WEDNESDAY
2	3	4	5
9	10	11	12
16	17	18	19
23	24	25	26
30	31		

THURSDAY	FRIDAY	SATURDAY	TO-DO LIST
		1	
6	7	8	
13	14	15	
20	21	22	
27	28	29	

MY WEEKLY PLANNER

MONDAY

TUESDAY

WEDNESDAY

THURSDAY

FRIDAY

SATURDAY

SUNDAY

MY NOTES

TO DO

-
-
-
-
-
-
-
-
-
-
-
-

MY WEEKLY PLANNER

MONDAY

TUESDAY

WEDNESDAY

THURSDAY

FRIDAY

SATURDAY

SUNDAY

TO DO

-
-
-
-
-
-
-
-
-
-
-
-

MY WEEKLY PLANNER

MONDAY	
TUESDAY	
WEDNESDAY	
THURSDAY	
FRIDAY	
SATURDAY	
SUNDAY	

MY NOTES

TO DO

-
-
-
-
-
-
-
-
-
-
-
-

MY WEEKLY PLANNER

MONDAY	
TUESDAY	
WEDNESDAY	
THURSDAY	
FRIDAY	
SATURDAY	
SUNDAY	

MY NOTES

TO DO

-
-
-
-
-
-
-
-
-
-
-
-

MY WEEKLY PLANNER

MONDAY

TUESDAY

WEDNESDAY

THURSDAY

FRIDAY

SATURDAY

SUNDAY

MY NOTES

TO DO

-
-
-
-
-
-
-
-
-
-
-

MY HABIT TRACKER

Cultivate positive change with this habit tracker. Log your daily habits for the month to stay focused and committed to achieving your goals. Fostering consistency and accountability helps to paves your path toward your aspirations

MONTH _____

HABIT:

1	2	3	4	5	6	7
8	9	10	11	12	13	14
15	16	17	18	19	20	21
22	23	24	25	26	27	28
29	30	31				

HABIT:

1	2	3	4	5	6	7
8	9	10	11	12	13	14
15	16	17	18	19	20	21
22	23	24	25	26	27	28
29	30	31				

HABIT:

1	2	3	4	5	6	7
8	9	10	11	12	13	14
15	16	17	18	19	20	21
22	23	24	25	26	27	28
29	30	31				

HABIT:

1	2	3	4	5	6	7
8	9	10	11	12	13	14
15	16	17	18	19	20	21
22	23	24	25	26	27	28
29	30	31				

HABIT:

1	2	3	4	5	6	7
8	9	10	11	12	13	14
15	16	17	18	19	20	21
22	23	24	25	26	27	28

HABIT:

1	2	3	4	5	6	7
8	9	10	11	12	13	14
15	16	17	18	19	20	21
22	23	24	25	26	27	28

MY MARCH REFLECTION

WHAT WENT WELL THIS MONTH?

WHAT DIDN'T GO SO WELL?

WHAT DID I DO FOR MY PHYSICAL AND MENTAL HEALTH THIS PAST MONTH?

1.
1.
3.
4.

WHAT AM I SPENDING TOO LITTLE AND TOO MUCH TIME ON?

WHAT AREAS OF MY LIFE DID I GROW THE MOST IN?

WHAT HAPPENED THIS MONTH MAKE ME FEEL THE MOST GRATEFUL?

1.
1.
3.
4.

WHAT CAN I ADJUST NEXT MONTH?

MY NOTES

"Oh, that you would bless me and enlarge my territory! Let your hand be with me, and keep me from harm so that I will be free from pain."

1 Chronicles 4:10

MY APRIL FOCUS

Begin your month with Intention.

Date

Intention

_____

_____

Annual goals	Positive Visualization
Things to Learn	Acts of Kindness

GRATITUDE

_____

_____

_____

APRIL 2025

SUNDAY	MONDAY	TUESDAY	WEDNESDAY
		1	2
6	7	8	9
13 Palm Sunday	14	15	16
20 Easter	21	22	23
27	28	29	30

54

THURSDAY	FRIDAY	SATURDAY	TO-DO LIST
3	4	5	
10	11	12	
17	18	19	
24	25	16	

MY WEEKLY PLANNER

MONDAY

TUESDAY

WEDNESDAY

THURSDAY

FRIDAY

SATURDAY

SUNDAY

MY NOTES

TO DO

-
-
-
-
-
-
-
-
-
-
-

MY WEEKLY PLANNER

MONDAY

TUESDAY

WEDNESDAY

THURSDAY

FRIDAY

SATURDAY

SUNDAY

MY NOTES

TO DO

MY WEEKLY PLANNER

MONDAY	
TUESDAY	
WEDNESDAY	
THURSDAY	
FRIDAY	
SATURDAY	
SUNDAY	

MY NOTES

TO DO

-
-
-
-
-
-
-
-
-
-
-
-

MY WEEKLY PLANNER

MONDAY

TUESDAY

WEDNESDAY

THURSDAY

FRIDAY

SATURDAY

SUNDAY

MY NOTES

TO DO

-
-
-
-
-
-
-
-
-
-
-
-

MY WEEKLY PLANNER

MONDAY

TUESDAY

WEDNESDAY

THURSDAY

FRIDAY

SATURDAY

SUNDAY

MY NOTES

TO DO

-
-
-
-
-
-
-
-
-
-
-
-

MY HABIT TRACKER

Cultivate positive change with this habit tracker. Log your daily habits for the month to stay focused and committed to achieving your goals. Fostering consistency and accountability helps to paves your path toward your aspirations

MONTH _____

HABIT:

1	2	3	4	5	6	7
8	9	10	11	12	13	14
15	16	17	18	19	20	21
22	23	24	25	26	27	28
29	30	31				

HABIT:

1	2	3	4	5	6	7
8	9	10	11	12	13	14
15	16	17	18	19	20	21
22	23	24	25	26	27	28
29	30	31				

HABIT:

1	2	3	4	5	6	7
8	9	10	11	12	13	14
15	16	17	18	19	20	21
22	23	24	25	26	27	28
29	30	31				

HABIT:

1	2	3	4	5	6	7
8	9	10	11	12	13	14
15	16	17	18	19	20	21
22	23	24	25	26	27	28
29	30	31				

HABIT:

1	2	3	4	5	6	7
8	9	10	11	12	13	14
15	16	17	18	19	20	21
22	23	24	25	26	27	28

HABIT:

1	2	3	4	5	6	7
8	9	10	11	12	13	14
15	16	17	18	19	20	21
22	23	24	25	26	27	28

MY APRIL REFLECTION

WHAT WENT WELL THIS MONTH?

WHAT DIDN'T GO SO WELL?

WHAT DID I DO FOR MY PHYSICAL AND MENTAL HEALTH THIS PAST MONTH?

1.
1.
3.
4.

WHAT AM I SPENDING TOO LITTLE AND TOO MUCH TIME ON?

WHAT AREAS OF MY LIFE DID I GROW THE MOST IN?

WHAT HAPPENED THIS MONTH MAKE ME FEEL THE MOST GRATEFUL?

1.
1.
3.
4.

WHAT CAN I ADJUST NEXT MONTH?

MY NOTES

"I press toward the goal for the prize of the upward call of God in Christ Jesus."

Philippians 3:14

MAY FOCUS

Begin your month with Intention.

Date

Intention

Annual goals

Positive Visualization

Things to Learn

Acts of Kindness

GRATITUDE

MAY 2025

SUNDAY	MONDAY	TUESDAY	WEDNESDAY
4	5	6	7
11	12	13	14
18	19	20	21
25	26 Memorial Day	27	28

THURSDAY	FRIDAY	SATURDAY	TO-DO LIST
1	2	3	
8	9	10	
15	16	17	
22	23	24	
29	30	31	

"I press toward the goal for the prize of the upward call of God in Christ Jesus." Philippians 3:14

67

MY WEEKLY PLANNER

MONDAY	
TUESDAY	
WEDNESDAY	
THURSDAY	
FRIDAY	
SATURDAY	
SUNDAY	

MY NOTES

TO DO

-
-
-
-
-
-
-
-
-
-
-
-

MY WEEKLY PLANNER

MONDAY	
TUESDAY	
WEDNESDAY	
THURSDAY	
FRIDAY	
SATURDAY	
SUNDAY	

MY NOTES

TO DO

-
-
-
-
-
-
-
-
-
-
-
-

MY WEEKLY PLANNER

MONDAY

TUESDAY

WEDNESDAY

THURSDAY

FRIDAY

SATURDAY

SUNDAY

MY NOTES

TO DO

-
-
-
-
-
-
-
-
-
-
-
-

MY WEEKLY PLANNER

MONDAY

TUESDAY

WEDNESDAY

THURSDAY

FRIDAY

SATURDAY

SUNDAY

MY NOTES

TO DO

-
-
-
-
-
-
-
-
-
-
-
-
-

MY WEEKLY PLANNER

MONDAY

TUESDAY

WEDNESDAY

THURSDAY

FRIDAY

SATURDAY

SUNDAY

MY NOTES

TO DO

-
-
-
-
-
-
-
-
-
-
-
-

MY HABIT TRACKER

Cultivate positive change with this habit tracker. Log your daily habits for the month to stay focused and committed to achieving your goals. Fostering consistency and accountability helps to paves your path toward your aspirations

MONTH _____

HABIT:

1	2	3	4	5	6	7
8	9	10	11	12	13	14
15	16	17	18	19	20	21
22	23	24	25	26	27	28
29	30	31				

HABIT:

1	2	3	4	5	6	7
8	9	10	11	12	13	14
15	16	17	18	19	20	21
22	23	24	25	26	27	28
29	30	31				

HABIT:

1	2	3	4	5	6	7
8	9	10	11	12	13	14
15	16	17	18	19	20	21
22	23	24	25	26	27	28
29	30	31				

HABIT:

1	2	3	4	5	6	7
8	9	10	11	12	13	14
15	16	17	18	19	20	21
22	23	24	25	26	27	28
29	30	31				

HABIT:

1	2	3	4	5	6	7
8	9	10	11	12	13	14
15	16	17	18	19	20	21
22	23	24	25	26	27	28

HABIT:

1	2	3	4	5	6	7
8	9	10	11	12	13	14
15	16	17	18	19	20	21
22	23	24	25	26	27	28

MY MAY REFLECTION

WHAT WENT WELL THIS MONTH?

WHAT DIDN'T GO SO WELL?

WHAT DID I DO FOR MY PHYSICAL AND MENTAL HEALTH THIS PAST MONTH?

1.
1.
3.
4.

WHAT AM I SPENDING TOO LITTLE AND TOO MUCH TIME ON?

WHAT AREAS OF MY LIFE DID I GROW THE MOST IN?

WHAT HAPPENED THIS MONTH MAKE ME FEEL THE MOST GRATEFUL?

1.
1.
3.
4.

WHAT CAN I ADJUST NEXT MONTH?

MY NOTES

"And we know that all things work together for good to them that love God, to them who are the called according to his purpose." Romans 8:28

MY JUNE FOCUS

Begin your month with Intention.

Date

Intention

Annual goals

Positive Visualization

Things to Learn

Acts of Kindness

GRATITUDE

JUNE 2025

SUNDAY	MONDAY	TUESDAY	WEDNESDAY
1	2	3	4
8	9	10	11
15	16	17	18
22	23	24	25
29	30		

things work together for good to them that love God, to them who are the called according to his purpose."   *Romans 8:28*

THURSDAY	FRIDAY	SATURDAY	TO-DO LIST
5	6	7	
12	13	14	
19 Juneteenth	20	21	
26	27	28	

MY WEEKLY PLANNER

MONDAY

TUESDAY

WEDNESDAY

THURSDAY

FRIDAY

SATURDAY

SUNDAY

TO DO

-
-
-
-
-
-
-
-
-
-
-
-

MY WEEKLY PLANNER

MONDAY	
TUESDAY	
WEDNESDAY	
THURSDAY	
FRIDAY	
SATURDAY	
SUNDAY	

TO DO

-
-
-
-
-
-
-
-
-
-
-

MY WEEKLY PLANNER

MONDAY	
TUESDAY	
WEDNESDAY	
THURSDAY	
FRIDAY	
SATURDAY	
SUNDAY	

MY NOTES

TO DO

-
-
-
-
-
-
-
-
-
-
-
-

MY WEEKLY PLANNER

MONDAY	
TUESDAY	
WEDNESDAY	
THURSDAY	
FRIDAY	
SATURDAY	
SUNDAY	

MY NOTES

TO DO

-
-
-
-
-
-
-
-
-
-
-
-

MY WEEKLY PLANNER

MONDAY

TUESDAY

WEDNESDAY

THURSDAY

FRIDAY

SATURDAY

SUNDAY

MY NOTES

TO DO

-
-
-
-
-
-
-
-
-
-
-
-

MY HABIT TRACKER

Cultivate positive change with this habit tracker. Log your daily habits for the month to stay focused and committed to achieving your goals. Fostering consistency and accountability helps to paves your path toward your aspirations

MONTH _____

HABIT:

1	2	3	4	5	6	7
8	9	10	11	12	13	14
15	16	17	18	19	20	21
22	23	24	25	26	27	28
29	30	31				

HABIT:

1	2	3	4	5	6	7
8	9	10	11	12	13	14
15	16	17	18	19	20	21
22	23	24	25	26	27	28
29	30	31				

HABIT:

1	2	3	4	5	6	7
8	9	10	11	12	13	14
15	16	17	18	19	20	21
22	23	24	25	26	27	28
29	30	31				

HABIT:

1	2	3	4	5	6	7
8	9	10	11	12	13	14
15	16	17	18	19	20	21
22	23	24	25	26	27	28
29	30	31				

HABIT:

1	2	3	4	5	6	7
8	9	10	11	12	13	14
15	16	17	18	19	20	21
22	23	24	25	26	27	28

HABIT:

1	2	3	4	5	6	7
8	9	10	11	12	13	14
15	16	17	18	19	20	21
22	23	24	25	26	27	28

MY JUNE REFLECTION

WHAT WENT WELL THIS MONTH?

WHAT DIDN'T GO SO WELL?

WHAT DID I DO FOR MY PHYSICAL AND MENTAL HEALTH THIS PAST MONTH?

1.

1.

3.

4.

WHAT AM I SPENDING TOO LITTLE AND TOO MUCH TIME ON?

WHAT AREAS OF MY LIFE DID I GROW THE MOST IN?

WHAT HAPPENED THIS MONTH MAKE ME FEEL THE MOST GRATEFUL?

1.

1.

3.

4.

WHAT CAN I ADJUST NEXT MONTH?

MY NOTES

In their hearts humans plan their course, but the Lord establishes their steps."

Proverbs 16:9

MY JULY FOCUS

Begin your month with Intention.

Date

Intention

Annual goals	Positive Visualization
Things to Learn	Acts of Kindness

GRATITUDE

JULY 2025

SUNDAY	MONDAY	TUESDAY	WEDNESDAY
		1	2
6	7	8	9
13	14	15	16
20	21	22	23
27	28	29	30

In their hearts humans plan their course, but the Lord establishes their steps." Proverbs 16:9

THURSDAY	FRIDAY	SATURDAY	TO-DO LIST
3	4 4th of July	5	
10	11	12	
17	18	19	
25	26	27	
31			

In their hearts humans plan their course, but the Lord establishes their steps." Proverbs 16:9

MY WEEKLY PLANNER

MONDAY

TUESDAY

WEDNESDAY

THURSDAY

FRIDAY

SATURDAY

SUNDAY

MY NOTES

TO DO

-
-
-
-
-
-
-
-
-
-
-

MY WEEKLY PLANNER

MONDAY	
TUESDAY	
WEDNESDAY	
THURSDAY	
FRIDAY	
SATURDAY	
SUNDAY	

MY NOTES

TO DO

-
-
-
-
-
-
-
-
-
-
-
-

MY WEEKLY PLANNER

MONDAY	
TUESDAY	
WEDNESDAY	
THURSDAY	
FRIDAY	
SATURDAY	
SUNDAY	

MY NOTES

TO DO

-
-
-
-
-
-
-
-
-
-
-
-

MY WEEKLY PLANNER

MONDAY

TUESDAY

WEDNESDAY

THURSDAY

FRIDAY

SATURDAY

SUNDAY

MY NOTES

TO DO

-
-
-
-
-
-
-
-
-
-
-
-

MY WEEKLY PLANNER

MONDAY	
TUESDAY	
WEDNESDAY	
THURSDAY	
FRIDAY	
SATURDAY	
SUNDAY	

MY NOTES

TO DO

-
-
-
-
-
-
-
-
-
-
-
-

MY HABIT TRACKER

Cultivate positive change with this habit tracker. Log your daily habits for the month to stay focused and committed to achieving your goals. Fostering consistency and accountability helps to paves your path toward your aspirations

MONTH _____

HABIT:

1	2	3	4	5	6	7
8	9	10	11	12	13	14
15	16	17	18	19	20	21
22	23	24	25	26	27	28
29	30	31				

HABIT:

1	2	3	4	5	6	7
8	9	10	11	12	13	14
15	16	17	18	19	20	21
22	23	24	25	26	27	28
29	30	31				

HABIT:

1	2	3	4	5	6	7
8	9	10	11	12	13	14
15	16	17	18	19	20	21
22	23	24	25	26	27	28
29	30	31				

HABIT:

1	2	3	4	5	6	7
8	9	10	11	12	13	14
15	16	17	18	19	20	21
22	23	24	25	26	27	28
29	30	31				

HABIT:

1	2	3	4	5	6	7
8	9	10	11	12	13	14
15	16	17	18	19	20	21
22	23	24	25	26	27	28

HABIT:

1	2	3	4	5	6	7
8	9	10	11	12	13	14
15	16	17	18	19	20	21
22	23	24	25	26	27	28

MY JULY REFLECTION

WHAT WENT WELL THIS MONTH?

WHAT DIDN'T GO SO WELL?

WHAT DID I DO FOR MY PHYSICAL AND MENTAL HEALTH THIS PAST MONTH?

1.
1.
3.
4.

WHAT AM I SPENDING TOO LITTLE AND TOO MUCH TIME ON?

WHAT AREAS OF MY LIFE DID I GROW THE MOST IN?

WHAT HAPPENED THIS MONTH MAKE ME FEEL THE MOST GRATEFUL?

1.
1.
3.
4.

WHAT CAN I ADJUST NEXT MONTH?

MY NOTES

"The Lord will guarantee a blessing on everything you do and will fill your storehouses with grain. The Lord your God will bless you in the land he is giving you."

Deuteronomy 28:8

MY AUGUST FOCUS

Begin your month with Intention.

Date

Intention

_____

_____

Annual goals	Positive Visualization
Things to Learn	Acts of Kindness

GRATITUDE

_____

_____

_____

AUGUST 2025

SUNDAY	MONDAY	TUESDAY	WEDNESDAY
3	4	5	6
10	11	12	13
17	18	19	20
24	25	26	27
31			

"The Lord will guarantee a blessing on everything you do... bless you in the land he is giving you." Deuteronomy 28:8

THURSDAY	FRIDAY	SATURDAY	TO-DO LIST
	1	2	
7	8	9	
14	15	16	
21	22	23	
28	29	30	

"The Lord will guarantee a blessing on everything you do... bless you in the land he is giving you." Deuteronomy 28:8

MY WEEKLY PLANNER

MONDAY

TUESDAY

WEDNESDAY

THURSDAY

FRIDAY

SATURDAY

SUNDAY

MY NOTES

TO DO

-
-
-
-
-
-
-
-
-
-
-
-

MY WEEKLY PLANNER

MONDAY	
TUESDAY	
WEDNESDAY	
THURSDAY	
FRIDAY	
SATURDAY	
SUNDAY	

MY NOTES

TO DO

-
-
-
-
-
-
-
-
-
-
-
-

MY WEEKLY PLANNER

MONDAY

TUESDAY

WEDNESDAY

THURSDAY

FRIDAY

SATURDAY

SUNDAY

TO DO

-
-
-
-
-
-
-
-
-
-
-
-

MY WEEKLY PLANNER

MONDAY	
TUESDAY	
WEDNESDAY	
THURSDAY	
FRIDAY	
SATURDAY	
SUNDAY	

MY NOTES

TO DO

-
-
-
-
-
-
-
-
-
-
-
-

MY WEEKLY PLANNER

MONDAY	
TUESDAY	
WEDNESDAY	
THURSDAY	
FRIDAY	
SATURDAY	
SUNDAY	

MY NOTES

TO DO

-
-
-
-
-
-
-
-
-
-
-
-

MY HABIT TRACKER

Cultivate positive change with this habit tracker. Log your daily habits for the month to stay focused and committed to achieving your goals. Fostering consistency and accountability helps to paves your path toward your aspirations

MONTH _____

HABIT:

1	2	3	4	5	6	7
8	9	10	11	12	13	14
15	16	17	18	19	20	21
22	23	24	25	26	27	28
29	30	31				

HABIT:

1	2	3	4	5	6	7
8	9	10	11	12	13	14
15	16	17	18	19	20	21
22	23	24	25	26	27	28
29	30	31				

HABIT:

1	2	3	4	5	6	7
8	9	10	11	12	13	14
15	16	17	18	19	20	21
22	23	24	25	26	27	28
29	30	31				

HABIT:

1	2	3	4	5	6	7
8	9	10	11	12	13	14
15	16	17	18	19	20	21
22	23	24	25	26	27	28
29	30	31				

HABIT:

1	2	3	4	5	6	7
8	9	10	11	12	13	14
15	16	17	18	19	20	21
22	23	24	25	26	27	28

HABIT:

1	2	3	4	5	6	7
8	9	10	11	12	13	14
15	16	17	18	19	20	21
22	23	24	25	26	27	28

MY AUGUST REFLECTION

WHAT WENT WELL THIS MONTH?

WHAT DIDN'T GO SO WELL?

WHAT DID I DO FOR MY PHYSICAL AND MENTAL HEALTH THIS PAST MONTH?

1.
1.
3.
4.

WHAT AM I SPENDING TOO LITTLE AND TOO MUCH TIME ON?

WHAT AREAS OF MY LIFE DID I GROW THE MOST IN?

WHAT HAPPENED THIS MONTH MAKE ME FEEL THE MOST GRATEFUL?

1.
1.
3.
4.

WHAT CAN I ADJUST NEXT MONTH?

MY NOTES

"With God's power working in us, God can do much more than anything we can ask or imagine."

Ephesians 3:20

MY SEPTEMBER FOCUS

Begin your month with Intention.

Date

Intention

_____

_____

Annual goals	Positive Visualization
Things to Learn	Acts of Kindness

GRATITUDE

_____

_____

_____

SEPTEMBER 2025

SUNDAY	MONDAY	TUESDAY	WEDNESDAY
	1 Labor Day	2	3
7	8	9	10
14	15	16	17
21	22	23	24
28	29	30	

THURSDAY	FRIDAY	SATURDAY	TO-DO LIST
4	5	6	
11	12	13	
18	19	20	
25	26	27	

MY WEEKLY PLANNER

MONDAY	
TUESDAY	
WEDNESDAY	
THURSDAY	
FRIDAY	
SATURDAY	
SUNDAY	

MY NOTES

TO DO

-
-
-
-
-
-
-
-
-
-
-
-

MY WEEKLY PLANNER

MONDAY	
TUESDAY	
WEDNESDAY	
THURSDAY	
FRIDAY	
SATURDAY	
SUNDAY	

MY NOTES

TO DO

- _____
- _____
- _____
- _____
- _____
- _____
- _____
- _____
- _____
- _____
- _____
- _____

MY WEEKLY PLANNER

MONDAY	
TUESDAY	
WEDNESDAY	
THURSDAY	
FRIDAY	
SATURDAY	
SUNDAY	

MY NOTES

TO DO

-
-
-
-
-
-
-
-
-
-
-
-

MY WEEKLY PLANNER

MONDAY	
TUESDAY	
WEDNESDAY	
THURSDAY	
FRIDAY	
SATURDAY	
SUNDAY	

MY NOTES

TO DO

-
-
-
-
-
-
-
-
-
-
-
-

MY WEEKLY PLANNER

MONDAY

TUESDAY

WEDNESDAY

THURSDAY

FRIDAY

SATURDAY

SUNDAY

MY NOTES

TO DO

-
-
-
-
-
-
-
-
-
-
-

MY HABIT TRACKER

Cultivate positive change with this habit tracker. Log your daily habits for the month to stay focused and committed to achieving your goals. Fostering consistency and accountability helps to paves your path toward your aspirations

MONTH _____

HABIT:

1	2	3	4	5	6	7
8	9	10	11	12	13	14
15	16	17	18	19	20	21
22	23	24	25	26	27	28
29	30	31				

HABIT:

1	2	3	4	5	6	7
8	9	10	11	12	13	14
15	16	17	18	19	20	21
22	23	24	25	26	27	28
29	30	31				

HABIT:

1	2	3	4	5	6	7
8	9	10	11	12	13	14
15	16	17	18	19	20	21
22	23	24	25	26	27	28
29	30	31				

HABIT:

1	2	3	4	5	6	7
8	9	10	11	12	13	14
15	16	17	18	19	20	21
22	23	24	25	26	27	28
29	30	31				

HABIT:

1	2	3	4	5	6	7
8	9	10	11	12	13	14
15	16	17	18	19	20	21
22	23	24	25	26	27	28

HABIT:

1	2	3	4	5	6	7
8	9	10	11	12	13	14
15	16	17	18	19	20	21
22	23	24	25	26	27	28

MY SEPTEMBER REFLECTION

WHAT WENT WELL THIS MONTH?

WHAT DIDN'T GO SO WELL?

WHAT DID I DO FOR MY PHYSICAL AND MENTAL HEALTH THIS PAST MONTH?

1.
1.
3.
4.

WHAT AM I SPENDING TOO LITTLE AND TOO MUCH TIME ON?

WHAT AREAS OF MY LIFE DID I GROW THE MOST IN?

WHAT HAPPENED THIS MONTH MAKE ME FEEL THE MOST GRATEFUL?

1.
1.
3.
4.

WHAT CAN I ADJUST NEXT MONTH?

MY NOTES

"May he give you the desire of your heart and make all your plans succeed."

Psalm 20:4

MY OCTOBER FOCUS

Begin your month with Intention.

Date

Intention

Annual goals	Positive Visualization
Things to Learn	Acts of Kindness

GRATITUDE

OCTOBER 2025

SUNDAY	MONDAY	TUESDAY	WEDNESDAY
			1
5	6	7	8
12	13 Indigeonous People's Day	14	15
19	20	21	22
26	27	28	29

THURSDAY	FRIDAY	SATURDAY	TO-DO LIST
2	3	4	
9	10	11	
16	17	18	
23	24	25	
30	31		

MY WEEKLY PLANNER

MONDAY	
TUESDAY	
WEDNESDAY	
THURSDAY	
FRIDAY	
SATURDAY	
SUNDAY	

MY NOTES

TO DO

- ....
- ....
- ....
- ....
- ....
- ....
- ....
- ....
- ....
- ....
- ....
- ....

MY WEEKLY PLANNER

MONDAY	
TUESDAY	
WEDNESDAY	
THURSDAY	
FRIDAY	
SATURDAY	
SUNDAY	

MY NOTES

TO DO

-
-
-
-
-
-
-
-
-
-
-
-

MY WEEKLY PLANNER

MONDAY

TUESDAY

WEDNESDAY

THURSDAY

FRIDAY

SATURDAY

SUNDAY

TO DO

-
-
-
-
-
-
-
-
-
-
-
-
-

MY WEEKLY PLANNER

MONDAY

TUESDAY

WEDNESDAY

THURSDAY

FRIDAY

SATURDAY

SUNDAY

MY NOTES

TO DO

-
-
-
-
-
-
-
-
-
-
-
-

MY WEEKLY PLANNER

MONDAY	
TUESDAY	
WEDNESDAY	
THURSDAY	
FRIDAY	
SATURDAY	
SUNDAY	

MY NOTES

_____

TO DO

- _____
- _____
- _____
- _____
- _____
- _____
- _____
- _____
- _____
- _____
- _____
- _____

MY HABIT TRACKER

Cultivate positive change with this habit tracker. Log your daily habits for the month to stay focused and committed to achieving your goals. Fostering consistency and accountability helps to paves your path toward your aspirations

MONTH _____

HABIT:

1	2	3	4	5	6	7
8	9	10	11	12	13	14
15	16	17	18	19	20	21
22	23	24	25	26	27	28
29	30	31				

HABIT:

1	2	3	4	5	6	7
8	9	10	11	12	13	14
15	16	17	18	19	20	21
22	23	24	25	26	27	28
29	30	31				

HABIT:

1	2	3	4	5	6	7
8	9	10	11	12	13	14
15	16	17	18	19	20	21
22	23	24	25	26	27	28
29	30	31				

HABIT:

1	2	3	4	5	6	7
8	9	10	11	12	13	14
15	16	17	18	19	20	21
22	23	24	25	26	27	28
29	30	31				

HABIT:

1	2	3	4	5	6	7
8	9	10	11	12	13	14
15	16	17	18	19	20	21
22	23	24	25	26	27	28

HABIT:

1	2	3	4	5	6	7
8	9	10	11	12	13	14
15	16	17	18	19	20	21
22	23	24	25	26	27	28

MY OCTOBER REFLECTION

WHAT WENT WELL THIS MONTH?

WHAT DIDN'T GO SO WELL?

WHAT DID I DO FOR MY PHYSICAL AND MENTAL HEALTH THIS PAST MONTH?

1.

1.

3.

4.

WHAT AM I SPENDING TOO LITTLE AND TOO MUCH TIME ON?

WHAT AREAS OF MY LIFE DID I GROW THE MOST IN?

WHAT HAPPENED THIS MONTH MAKE ME FEEL THE MOST GRATEFUL?

1.

1.

3.

4.

WHAT CAN I ADJUST NEXT MONTH?

MY NOTES

"In all your ways acknowledge Him, And He shall direct your paths."

Proverbs 3:6

MY NOVEMBER FOCUS

Begin your month with Intention.

Date

Intention

Annual goals	Positive Visualization
Things to Learn	Acts of Kindness

GRATITUDE

NOVEMBER

SUNDAY	MONDAY	TUESDAY	WEDNESDAY
2	3	4	5
9	10	11 Veterans Day	12
16	17	18	19
23	24	25	26
30			

THURSDAY	FRIDAY	SATURDAY	TO-DO LIST
		1	
6	7	8	
13	14	15	
20	21	22	
27 Thanksgiving Day	28	29	

MY WEEKLY PLANNER

MONDAY	
TUESDAY	
WEDNESDAY	
THURSDAY	
FRIDAY	
SATURDAY	
SUNDAY	

MY NOTES

TO DO

-
-
-
-
-
-
-
-
-
-
-
-

MY WEEKLY PLANNER

MONDAY

TUESDAY

WEDNESDAY

THURSDAY

FRIDAY

SATURDAY

SUNDAY

MY NOTES

TO DO

-
-
-
-
-
-
-
-
-
-
-
-

MY WEEKLY PLANNER

MONDAY

TUESDAY

WEDNESDAY

THURSDAY

FRIDAY

SATURDAY

SUNDAY

MY NOTES

TO DO

-
-
-
-
-
-
-
-
-
-
-
-

MY WEEKLY PLANNER

MONDAY	
TUESDAY	
WEDNESDAY	
THURSDAY	
FRIDAY	
SATURDAY	
SUNDAY	

TO DO

-
-
-
-
-
-
-
-
-
-
-
-

MY WEEKLY PLANNER

MONDAY	
TUESDAY	
WEDNESDAY	
THURSDAY	
FRIDAY	
SATURDAY	
SUNDAY	

MY NOTES

TO DO

-
-
-
-
-
-
-
-
-
-
-

MY HABIT TRACKER

Cultivate positive change with this habit tracker. Log your daily habits for the month to stay focused and committed to achieving your goals. Fostering consistency and accountability helps to paves your path toward your aspirations

MONTH _____

HABIT:

1	2	3	4	5	6	7
8	9	10	11	12	13	14
15	16	17	18	19	20	21
22	23	24	25	26	27	28
29	30	31				

HABIT:

1	2	3	4	5	6	7
8	9	10	11	12	13	14
15	16	17	18	19	20	21
22	23	24	25	26	27	28
29	30	31				

HABIT:

1	2	3	4	5	6	7
8	9	10	11	12	13	14
15	16	17	18	19	20	21
22	23	24	25	26	27	28
29	30	31				

HABIT:

1	2	3	4	5	6	7
8	9	10	11	12	13	14
15	16	17	18	19	20	21
22	23	24	25	26	27	28
29	30	31				

HABIT:

1	2	3	4	5	6	7
8	9	10	11	12	13	14
15	16	17	18	19	20	21
22	23	24	25	26	27	28

HABIT:

1	2	3	4	5	6	7
8	9	10	11	12	13	14
15	16	17	18	19	20	21
22	23	24	25	26	27	28

MY NOVEMBER REFLECTION

WHAT WENT WELL THIS MONTH?

WHAT DIDN'T GO SO WELL?

WHAT DID I DO FOR MY PHYSICAL AND MENTAL HEALTH THIS PAST MONTH?

1.
1.
3.
4.

WHAT AM I SPENDING TOO LITTLE AND TOO MUCH TIME ON?

WHAT AREAS OF MY LIFE DID I GROW THE MOST IN?

WHAT HAPPENED THIS MONTH MAKE ME FEEL THE MOST GRATEFUL?

1.
1.
3.
4.

WHAT CAN I ADJUST NEXT MONTH?

MY NOTES

"Without counsel plans fail, but with many advisers they succeed."

Proverbs 15:22

MY DECEMBER FOCUS

Begin your month with Intention.

Date

Intention

_____

_____

Annual goals	Positive Visualization
Things to Learn	Acts of Kindness

GRATITUDE

_____

_____

_____

DECEMBER 2025

SUNDAY	MONDAY	TUESDAY	WEDNESDAY
	1	2	3
7	8	9	10
14	15	16	17
21	22	23	24 Christmas Eve
28 Kwanzaa	29 Kwanzaa	30 Kwanzaa	31 New Years Eve Kwanzaa

150

THURSDAY	FRIDAY	SATURDAY	TO-DO LIST
4	5	6	
11	12	13	
18	19	20	
25 Christmas Day	26 Kwanzaa	27 Kwanzaa	

MY WEEKLY PLANNER

MONDAY

TUESDAY

WEDNESDAY

THURSDAY

FRIDAY

SATURDAY

SUNDAY

MY NOTES

TO DO

-
-
-
-
-
-
-
-
-
-
-
-

MY WEEKLY PLANNER

MONDAY	
TUESDAY	
WEDNESDAY	
THURSDAY	
FRIDAY	
SATURDAY	
SUNDAY	

MY NOTES

TO DO

-
-
-
-
-
-
-
-
-
-
-
-
-

MY WEEKLY PLANNER

MONDAY

TUESDAY

WEDNESDAY

THURSDAY

FRIDAY

SATURDAY

SUNDAY

MY NOTES

TO DO

-
-
-
-
-
-
-
-
-
-
-

MY WEEKLY PLANNER

MONDAY	
TUESDAY	
WEDNESDAY	
THURSDAY	
FRIDAY	
SATURDAY	
SUNDAY	

MY NOTES

TO DO

-
-
-
-
-
-
-
-
-
-
-
-

MY WEEKLY PLANNER

MONDAY	
TUESDAY	
WEDNESDAY	
THURSDAY	
FRIDAY	
SATURDAY	
SUNDAY	

MY NOTES

TO DO

-
-
-
-
-
-
-
-
-
-
-

MY HABIT TRACKER

Cultivate positive change with this habit tracker. Log your daily habits for the month to stay focused and committed to achieving your goals. Fostering consistency and accountability helps to paves your path toward your aspirations

MONTH _____

HABIT:

1	2	3	4	5	6	7
8	9	10	11	12	13	14
15	16	17	18	19	20	21
22	23	24	25	26	27	28
29	30	31				

HABIT:

1	2	3	4	5	6	7
8	9	10	11	12	13	14
15	16	17	18	19	20	21
22	23	24	25	26	27	28
29	30	31				

HABIT:

1	2	3	4	5	6	7
8	9	10	11	12	13	14
15	16	17	18	19	20	21
22	23	24	25	26	27	28
29	30	31				

HABIT:

1	2	3	4	5	6	7
8	9	10	11	12	13	14
15	16	17	18	19	20	21
22	23	24	25	26	27	28
29	30	31				

HABIT:

1	2	3	4	5	6	7
8	9	10	11	12	13	14
15	16	17	18	19	20	21
22	23	24	25	26	27	28

HABIT:

1	2	3	4	5	6	7
8	9	10	11	12	13	14
15	16	17	18	19	20	21
22	23	24	25	26	27	28

MY DECEMBER REFLECTION

WHAT WENT WELL THIS MONTH?

WHAT DIDN'T GO SO WELL?

WHAT DID I DO FOR MY PHYSICAL AND MENTAL HEALTH THIS PAST MONTH?

1.
1.
3.
4.

WHAT AM I SPENDING TOO LITTLE AND TOO MUCH TIME ON?

WHAT AREAS OF MY LIFE DID I GROW THE MOST IN?

WHAT HAPPENED THIS MONTH MAKE ME FEEL THE MOST GRATEFUL?

1.
1.
3.
4.

WHAT CAN I ADJUST NEXT MONTH?

MY NOTES

"The Lord has done great things for us, and we are filled with joy."

Psalm 126:3

2025 REFLECTION

WHAT WENT WELL THIS YEAR?

WHAT DIDN'T GO SO WELL?

WHAT IS THE MOST IMPORTANT LESSON YOU LEARNED THIS YEAR?

WHAT CHALLENGES DID YOU OVERCOME?

WHAT IS THE BEST THING THAT HAPPENED?

HOW DID YOU TAKE CARE OF YOURSELF THIS YEAR?

WHAT ARE YOU THANKFUL FOR THIS YEAR?

MY NOTES

JAN

S	M	T	W	T	F	S
				1	2	3
4	5	6	7	8	9	10
11	12	13	14	15	16	17
18	19	20	21	22	23	24
25	26	27	28	29	30	31

FEB

S	M	T	W	T	F	S
1	2	3	4	5	6	7
8	9	10	11	12	13	14
15	16	17	18	19	20	21
22	23	24	25	26	27	28

MAR

S	M	T	W	T	F	S
1	2	3	4	5	6	7
8	9	10	11	12	13	14
15	16	17	18	19	20	21
22	23	24	25	26	27	28
29	30	31				

APR

S	M	T	W	T	F	S
			1	2	3	4
5	6	7	8	9	10	11
12	13	14	15	16	17	18
19	20	21	22	23	24	25
26	27	28	29	30		

MAY

S	M	T	W	T	F	S
					1	2
3	4	5	6	7	8	9
10	11	12	13	14	15	16
17	18	19	20	21	22	23
24	25	26	27	28	29	30
31						

JUN

S	M	T	W	T	F	S
	1	2	3	4	5	6
7	8	9	10	11	12	13
14	15	16	17	18	19	20
21	22	23	24	25	26	27
28	29	30				

JUL

S	M	T	W	T	F	S
			1	2	3	4
5	6	7	8	9	10	11
12	13	14	15	16	17	18
19	20	21	22	23	24	25
26	27	28	29	30	31	

AUG

S	M	T	W	T	F	S
						1
2	3	4	5	6	7	8
9	10	11	12	13	14	15
16	17	18	19	20	21	22
23	24	25	26	27	28	29
30	31					

SEP

S	M	T	W	T	F	S
		1	2	3	4	5
6	7	8	9	10	11	12
13	14	15	16	17	18	19
20	21	22	23	24	25	26
27	28	29	30			

OCT

S	M	T	W	T	F	S
				1	2	3
4	5	6	7	8	9	10
11	12	13	14	15	16	17
18	19	20	21	22	23	24
25	26	27	28	29	30	31

NOV

S	M	T	W	T	F	S
1	2	3	4	5	6	7
8	9	10	11	12	13	14
15	16	17	18	19	20	21
22	23	24	25	26	27	28
29	30					

DEC

S	M	T	W	T	F	S
		1	2	3	4	5
6	7	8	9	10	11	12
13	14	15	16	17	18	19
20	21	22	23	24	25	26
27	28	29	30	31		

Made in the USA
Las Vegas, NV
28 January 2025

17112473R00092